D0931590

MUD BOOK
by
JOHN CAGE
AND
LOIS LONG

MUD BOOK

How To Make Pies and Cakes

By John Cage and Lois Long
With a Note by John Russell

HARRY N. ABRAMS, INC., PUBLISHERS, NEW YORK

MUD PIE

SOME DIRT AND

ENOUGH   WATER

MIX DIRT AND WATER
UNTIL IT STAYS
WHERE EVER
YOU PUT IT   INSTEAD OF RUNNING THE WAY WATER

IF IT IS TOO SLOPPY—

SQUEEZE IT

UNTIL SOME OF THE WATER GETS OUT

DUMP IT ONTO A NEWSPAPER

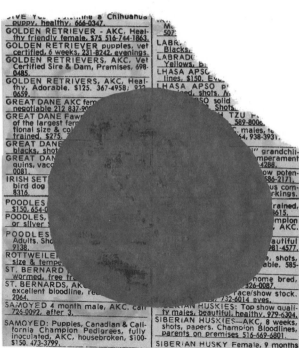

BAKE OUTDOORS
IN SUNSHINE
WHERE NOTHING
IS DRIPPING

MUD LAYER CAKE

SIFT

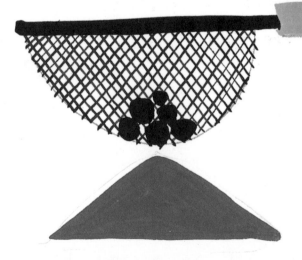

DIRT

DON'T LET ANY PEBBLES
STAY IN THE DIRT — BUT
SAVE THEM BECAUSE YOU
WILL NEED THEM LATER.

IF DIRT WILL NOT SIFT

STEP ON IT   OR

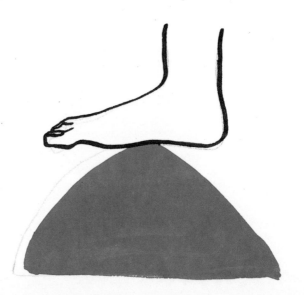

POUND IT WITH A STONE

STOP SIFTING

WHEN YOU HAVE FOUR CUPS OF DIRT.

IF YOU DIDN'T GET A CUP OF PEBBLES OUT OF THE DIRT . . . . HUNT FOR MORE UNTIL YOU HAVE A CUP FULL . .

4 CUPS OF DIRT AND 2 CUPS OF WATER
WILL MAKE GOOD MUD, UNLESS YOUR DIRT
IS DUSTY — THEN YOU MIGHT NEED MORE WATER.

IF IT HAS JUST RAINED YOU MIGHT NOT
NEED ANY WATER AT ALL BECAUSE YOUR
DIRT WILL ALREADY HAVE IT IN IT...

MIX THE DIRT WITH THE WATE

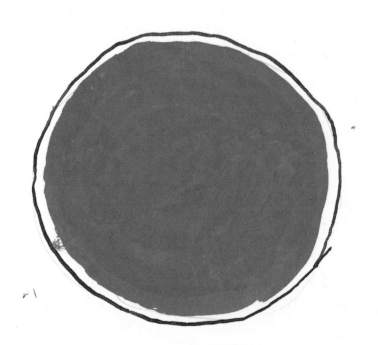

UT THE OTHER HALF IN ANOTHER PIE PAN

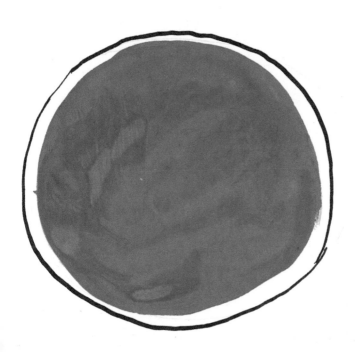

SET THEM IN THE SUN TO BAK

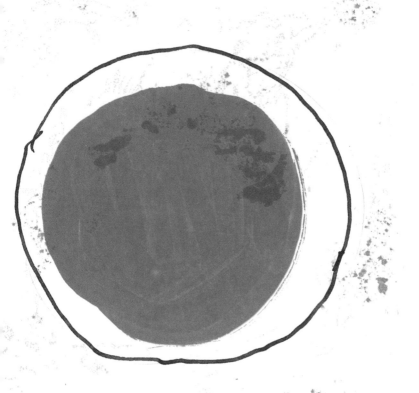

NTIL THE PIE GETS SMALLER THAN THE PAN

PUT A PIECE OF CARDBOARD ON TOP
OF THE PIE

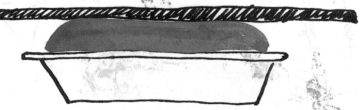

TURN IT UPSIDE DOWN

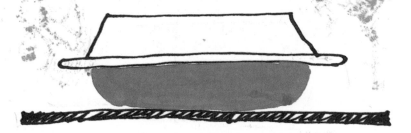

TAKE AWAY THE ~~PLATE~~ PAN

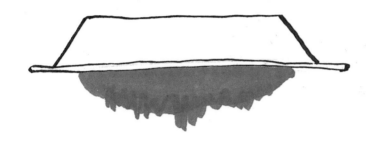

IF IT STICKS IT'S NOT DONE
YOU HAVE TO WAIT MORE

PUT A PLATE
ON TOP OF THE
OTHER PIE ___ HOLDING THEM TOGET

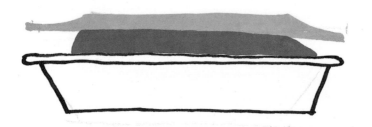

TURN THEM BOTH OVER ___ SO THAT

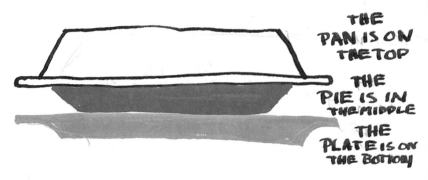

THE
PAN IS ON
THE TOP

THE
PIE IS IN
THE MIDDLE

THE
PLATE IS ON
THE BOTTOM

LIKEASANDWICH

REMOVE THE PAN
GET THE PEBBLES
AND QUICKLY PRESS THEM
INTO THE TOP OF THE PIE
YOU MUST FINISH BEFORE
THE PIE IS DRY OR THEY
WILL JUST ROLL OFF.

PUT THE FIRST PIE
ON TOP OF THE PEBBLES

IF IT CRACKS — PUT A LITTLE WATER IN
THE CRACK AND PUSH IT BACK TOGETHER

FOR A BIRTHDAY CAKE

DANDELIONS

MAKE NICE CANDLES IF THEY ARE DRIED U

MAKE A WISH

AND BLOW OUT ALL THE CANDLES

MUD PIES ARE TO MAKE

AND TO LOOK AT

NOT TO EAT

A Note on "Mud Book"

Behind the great pies of history — the eel pie, the oyster pie, the pumpkin pie, the Christmas pie and that henchman of cardiac arrest, the Mississippi Mud Pie — there stands the humble and inedible ancestor that is the subject of this book.

For what is the mud pie

if not the proto-pie, first fruit of
the primal ooze? And what is
the making of mud pies if not the
first working model of all human
makings?

But it took John Cage to see
that, just as it took John Cage
to release the music so long
sealed up in silence.

And it took Lois Long to let

the sunlight and make the candles
arkle like starshell.

So let's hear it for Lois and John,
ho twenty and some years ago
at down after dinner in Pomona,
ew York, and proved that a good
nd pie, like a good anything else,
lls for feeling and imagination,
re thought and love.

John Russell
September 1981

Editor: Charles Miers
Designer: Samuel N. Antupit

Library of Congress Cataloging in Publication Number: 88–70773
ISBN 0-8109-1533-2
Copyright © 1983 by John Cage and Lois Long

Published in 1988 by Harry N. Abrams, Incorporated, New York.
All rights reserved. No parts of the contents of this book
may be reproduced without the written permission of the publisher

A Times Mirror Company

Printed and bound in Japan

AFTERWORD

Having had the pleasure of taking charge of the American distribution of the limited-edition *Mud Book,* it gives me great pleasure to see this treasure become available to a wider audience.

One fall evening during the mid-1950s (the artists themselves cannot remember the exact year), the original drawings and text for the *Mud Book* were made in a flurry of intense creative activity. The maquette was put away without much further thought until Lois Long rediscovered it in her files and showed it to fellow artist Graham Snow, who in turn showed it to his dealer, the prominent London gallery owner David Grob.

Grob's immediate enthusiasm resulted in a collaboration with the renowned printer Hiroshi Kawanishi of Simca Print Artists in Tokyo. Together they produced the *Mud Book* in a limited edition of 500 signed and numbered copies. Simca, widely known for making outstanding print publications with artists, including Jasper Johns, Alex Katz, and Jennifer Bartlett, translated the original illustrations and text into silk-screen prints. Using over 100 screens, they matched the original with rarely seen fidelity and sensitivity.

All of those involved with the original publication of the *Mud Book* are pleased that Abrams has taken the care to preserve the feeling and integrity of the original in this popular edition.

Joe Fawbush
Fawbush Gallery, New York

THE AUTHORS

John Cage was born in Los Angeles in 1912. He studied music under Henry Cowell and Arnold Schönberg before becoming musical director of the Merce Cunningham Dance Company in 1943. He has since revolutionized the parameters of music, experimenting with everyday objects (from tin cans to clothespins) as his instruments and incorporating elements of chance into his compositions. He is credited with conducting the first Happening, at Black Mountain College in 1952, and is internationally celebrated for his critical writings, his poetry, and his prolific work in the graphic arts.

Lois Long was born in Clarksdale, Mississippi, in 1918. She studied design and later taught at Pratt Institute in New York. Currently a textile designer in Manhattan, she has created several books, including another collaboration with John Cage entitled *Mushroom Book,* in which she and Cage were able to indulge their prodigious knowledge of fungi.